Concerning the Importance
of God for Mental Health

# Concerning the Importance of God for Mental Health

RELIGIOUS FAITH AND ITS RELATIONSHIP TO LONG-TERM COGNITIVE, EMOTIONAL, AND BEHAVIORAL OUTCOMES

Marcia A. Murphy

RESOURCE *Publications* • Eugene, Oregon

CONCERNING THE IMPORTANCE OF GOD FOR MENTAL HEALTH
Religious Faith and Its Relationship to Long-Term Cognitive, Emotional, and Behavioral Outcomes

Copyright © 2025 Marcia A. Murphy. All rights reserved. Except for brief quotations in critical publications or reviews, no part of this book may be reproduced in any manner without prior written permission from the publisher. Write: Permissions, Wipf and Stock Publishers, 199 W. 8th Ave., Suite 3, Eugene, OR 97401.

Resource Publications
An Imprint of Wipf and Stock Publishers
199 W. 8th Ave., Suite 3
Eugene, OR 97401

www.wipfandstock.com

PAPERBACK ISBN: 979-8-3852-3493-6
HARDCOVER ISBN: 979-8-3852-3494-3
EBOOK ISBN: 979-8-3852-3495-0

VERSION NUMBER 03/13/25

Scripture quotations marked (ESV) are from The Holy Bible, English Standard Version (ESV), copyright ©2001 by Crossway Bibles, a publishing ministry of Good News Publishers. Used by permission. All rights reserved.

Scripture quotations marked (NIV) are taken from the Holy Bible, New International Version®, NIV®. Copyright © 1973, 1978, 1984, 2011 by Biblica, Inc.™ Used by permission of Zondervan. All rights reserved worldwide. www.zondervan.com. The "NIV" and "New International Version" are trademarks registered in the United States Patent and Trademark Office by Biblica, Inc.™

Scripture quotations marked (RSV) are from the Revised Standard Version of the Bible, copyright © 1946, 1952, and 1971 National Council of the Churches of Christ in the United States of America. Used by permission. All rights reserved worldwide.

The author wishes to thank Kelly G. Wilson, PhD, University of Mississippi, for permission granted to use the Valued Living Questionnaire for her research, November 8, 2024.

To all those who seek the ways of
truth, love, and justice

Love is not a weak, spineless emotion;
it is a powerful, moral force on the side of justice.

BERNICE A. KING

# Contents

*Preface* | ix
*Acknowledgments* | xiii
*Author's Note* | xiv

**I. When Psychiatry/Psychology/Religion Meet**
   Personal Encounter with the Lord | 3
   Other's Experience of God | 9
   Religious Claims | 12

**II. Influence of Long-Term Christian Faith on Character Development**
   Values/Traits/Purpose in life | 19
   Daily Life: When Faith Makes a Difference | 42

**III. Partners/Therapeutic Process**
   Religious Pluralism and Therapy | 47

Conclusion | 51

*Appendix: Further Reading* | 59
*Bibliography* | 63

# Preface

BEING BORN AND RAISED in the United States of America, I make a case for how the acknowledgment of spiritual factors in psychiatric recovery are long overdue in this part of the world, both, in academia and clinical practice. A Midwestern, senior psychiatric academic healthcare provider states that this kind of discussion rarely occurs in the US (as of 2024). Being in the recovery process from a psychotic disorder, including schizophrenia, PTSD, and clinical depression, I share personal experience of how faith has the potential to improve the quality of our lives. Faith can contribute to healthy mindsets and lifestyles.

The development of personality traits and subsequently, lifestyles, has a basis in more than genetics. Genetics may play a part but there is more. Current research being done in this area appears to be reductionistic and oversimplified. I tackle questions in different ways, from a viewpoint stressing the complexity of the human organism as body, brain—and as my book additionally maintains—spirit. I am not a scientist but am, instead, exploring the psychology of religion in relation to mental health. My work explores the question: what is the importance of God and theology in relation to cognitive , emotional, and behavioral outcomes? When it comes to science and religion it is not a question of either/or; but of both/and. No binary choice is required; instead, there can be a more holistic and inclusive paradigm as each side will interact with and influence the other.

## Preface

I maintain that the development of personality is primarily dependent on values, spiritual values, instilled since birth and throughout the growing years primarily through environmental/social means along with individual choice. A belief in God is not caused by one's genes. Religion is an individual choice which can be supported and strengthened by religious exercises such as church/temple attendance, reading of sacred texts, and prayer.

The following topics are explored in this book from a patient's perspective with support from personal research and religious community: What is the relationship between religion and cognition? Between religion and emotion? Between religion and actions/behavior? I explore the possible outcomes of a Judeo-Christian faith on these three categories and, additionally, how is moral psychology influenced by religious belief? Which leads us to the role of personal values and how character development is influenced by long-term religious practice. I also touch upon how being humane, the psychology of compassion, has an impact on the quality of daily life for oneself, and for others. And, finally, what is Religiously-Integrated Cognitive Behavioral Therapy (RCBT) with the complex problem of religious pluralism in clinical practice.

The reality of human death is something many people try to ignore in their daily life. But what happens after death is of great significance. We will all pass away. Personally, this thought is a bit scary. Will our consciousness cease to exist also? Or will there still be thinking, feeling, and an awareness of our surroundings? The concept of eternal life is attractive because I would rather be alive than dead for eternity. Is there something that offers eternal life? Some religions teach this. But which religion is true and which is false? And how does this question influence our daily thought processes, activities, and goals? Which faith tradition can provide comfort and peace? Which produces anxiety? Some people may try to deaden their fears with alcohol and illicit drug use or love affairs to try to escape the big questions. But is it possible to escape? I have to answer, no, it isn't. There is no escape.

Now you might ask: What does all this have to do with mental health? I answer: Everything. Our response or lack of response to

## Preface

the big and deeper questions influence the trajectory of our daily lives i.e., how we think, feel, and act. It affects the way we treat others and even how we treat ourselves. It determines our goals and ambitions or lack thereof. How we deal with stress and tragedy is directly an outcome of our view of the big picture, whether we are resilient or crumble under pressure. Our morality is also largely determined by our view of the big picture, what we think of in terms of personal ethical choices. The list goes on.

In this book I give a glimpse of my view of the big picture, partly what I learned as a psychiatric patient who was almost completely destroyed by psychosis. With the help of counselors, physicians, and a faith community a broken life, shattered to pieces at one point, became somewhat rebuilt, and restored. Sure, I can't say I have a perfect life now, but it is one filled with meaningful work and new friendships. To develop my theme I also give a glimpse of other's lives who've I met along my journey, people who answered questionnaires I mailed out and who participated in interviews. The general ideas arising from the analysis of these exercises help us to go deeper in thought about the big questions in life that, in addition, can improve the quality of our lives. I found priorities of the participants for what they value most in life. People who responded in my research are examples of those who did well with their choices and who produced fruitful and meaningful lives. What can we learn from them, their examples? And what can the field of psychiatry learn from them to improve the therapeutic process for their patients?

Personally, I have received a lot of excellent psychiatric care in a hospital out-patient clinic in the Midwest. But, generally speaking, the way psychiatric care has been provided across a large part of the US in the past several decades has been a travesty: fifteen-minute *med checks*. Little psychotherapy or counseling. The state of Iowa has been a low-access area where there is great need and very few psychiatrists. Psychiatrists attempt to decipher within a few minutes if the medications are being administered in a correct manner based on whether patients have any overt symptoms or if they are suicidal. That has been the gest of it. And appointments are only every few months of the year. Nothing in depth, no real therapy, just seeing if the drugs are working and in some cases they are not. Sure, there are a few exceptions when patients' conditions improve, but the chances of success are not in their favor. Why? Because psychiatric care needs to go deeper, psychologically, and spiritually. Patients need to be able to share more of their lives, what they do day to day and how they think about life circumstances—share their thoughts and feelings about what they value, long for, and strive for that gives their life meaning. Few psychiatric clinics in low-access areas have enough professionals to offer patients appointment time to do this; there is a shortage of counselors and psychologists. Or it may be that only those patients with financial means can pay to obtain the type of therapist who can provide sessions of a greater length, sort of—money buys time. The lower-income psychiatric patient gets lost in the shuffle or are sometimes discarded which is a whole other story.

If a psychiatric clinic is totally controlled by insurance companies, then there really is no hope. What we need are physicians and administrators to stand their ground and defend the patient who needs adequate in-depth care. Having hope for future changes in the system I offer this book as something from a patient's perspective for how counseling and management of symptoms can enter the realm of the spiritual or in-depth care—which is reaching deeper into what really makes us human—a far contrast to the fifteen-minute med check. I address meaningful topics that touch upon what makes life worth living. And as for the general reader who may have picked up this book out of curiosity, perhaps there are insights which can enrich and improve the quality of our everyday lives.

# Acknowledgments

I AM GRATEFUL TO many people who supported my writing of this book: The Saint Andrew Presbyterian Church Prayer Ministry Group of Iowa City, Iowa; the entire Mental Health Initiatives (MHI) program's past and current team members, including the Group for the Advancement of Mental Health (GAMH) who have been unwavering in their work as advocates for the mentally ill. I am especially grateful for the continuous support I've received from the Mission, Outreach, and Service (MOS) team and the rest of my church family and friends at Saint Andrew. Thank you to all of these individuals and groups.

# Author's Note

This is nonfiction.
The following stories are true events
along with the accompanying information

# I

# When Psychiatry/Psychology/Religion Meet

# Personal Encounter with the Lord

> The voice of the Lord is over the waters;
> the God of glory thunders,
> the Lord, over many waters.
> The voice of the Lord is powerful;
> the voice of the Lord is full of majesty.
>
> *PSALM 29:3–4 ESV*

MY EXPERIENCE OF HEARING God's voice occurred when I was in my early twenties, in a suburb of New York City. It would probably be helpful if I defined what I mean by *God*. I grew up in the Midwestern US, in a Lutheran (ELCA) Christian denomination. It's known to be less strict than its cousin, the LCMS. For example, the pastor from my church joined protestors marching down the city streets during the Viet Nam war. He allowed homeless people to sleep in the church building. As a teen I was drawn to the Unitarian Universalist Society which is not really a church, but a group of people who gather to discuss various issues and viewpoints. My Christian upbringing taught me about the Holy Trinity being: God the Father, Son, and Holy Spirit. After years of traumatic struggles when I was in my thirties, I attended Roman Catholic masses at a local church and joined that faith tradition. And eventually I transferred over to The Presbyterian Church (USA), where I am today.

## Concerning the Importance of God for Mental Health

My religious beliefs have had as its basis the biblical teachings about who God is in the Trinity: God the Father, Son, and Holy Spirit. My personal faith is conservatively biblical, not New Age or post-Christian (God as *she*). My faith is grounded in both the Old and New Testaments with deep roots in Exodus, the Ten Commandments, and the prophetic witnesses of God's ancient people as recorded in the books: Isaiah, Jeremiah, Amos, Hosea, Ezekiel, etc.; and as recorded in the New Testament gospel of John, Jesus Christ referred to God as his Father. I see Christ as my Divine authority and, along with the other New and Old Testament writings, will always refer to God as the Trinity: Father, Son, and Holy Spirit.

My biological family was middle-class and my parents worked hard. Even though they brought the family to church the home life was still full of strife. My younger brother had epilepsy as well as violent behavior issues and he made some attempts to kill me so I never felt safe. This situation caused feelings of insecurity, anxiety, and depression. I also did not get along with my mother. I had few friends. Amongst all family members there was daily bickering. My parents eventually divorced. In later years, alcohol mis-use was prevalent in my siblings and one parent and their behaviors were subsequently morally reprehensible.

Early on in life before the age of five, I began to hear voices, once what I thought was a witch in the attic as I tried to get to sleep at night. Later, as a teen, I turned self-destructive with self-cutting on my wrist and arms with razor blades. Eventually, I over-dosed on a bottle of Bayer aspirin and the hospital emergency department saved my life.

Before these major mental health problems emerged, I ran for office in the middle school Round Table (the student council) and was elected the first female president in the school's history. I was on the senior high tennis team and upon graduation a University retired tennis coach invited me to work out with tennis pros in California. I was unable to afford the expense and then this coach offered me a job of teaching tennis in the small town of Osceola, Iowa. There I boarded with a retired nurse and held daily classes for children, teens, and adults at the neighborhood school's tennis courts. This was a lot of responsibility for a young eighteen-year-old and the loneliness I endured was crushing. This appointment was only for one summer and returning home I attended a few college classes with the money I had earned teaching tennis while living with my divorced dad and older brother. They mostly kept to themselves with few words exchanged.

In February 1973, a little before my nineteenth birthday, I ended up joining in a quasi-religious cult which was not Christian. Though called the Unification Church it was not really a church but was an organization with the goal of making the leaders wealthy; all the leaders cared about was money and becoming rich. The founder of the cult had no scruples, no conscience whatsoever, even sacrificing the safety and lives of its members. All the leaders of this cult whether locally, nationally, or internationally, were morally reprehensible and wicked. Many cult members got swept away or killed, and never returned home. I was one of the lucky ones who escaped.

During the cult years I was entirely chaste, and became obsessed with God, and finally became psychotic. It was during a rainstorm with thunder, lightning, and a downpour that God spoke to me. The psychosis I had been enduring for about eighteen months enveloped me in demonic forces, evil spirits threatening and accusing me. These supernatural voices were not inside my head, they surrounded me from whatever room environment I happened to be in or even outdoors. They tried to make me kill myself, once by telling me to jump out of a twenty-story window of a building in downtown Manhattan. I was in extreme fear. Later cult leaders forced me to stay at a cult center in a small suburb of New York City. It was there during an evening thunderstorm I felt compelled to get up out of my sleeping bag I had been trying to sleep in on the floor. Demons had been surrounding me in the room, yelling obscenities into my ears, some coming from the floor beneath my head as I lay down; and I was in an emotional state of terror. The demons' voices were not in my head. It was like Jesus hearing the devil talking while he was in the desert and was not inside Jesus's head. A while later, my psychiatrist, Dr. Russell

Noyes Jr., told me this (that my experience was like Jesus's) and I had already come to a previously independent and similar conclusion. See Matt 4:1–11, for the way Jesus heard the devil speaking to him.

I quickly went over to an open bay window. I looked outside toward the murky darkness of cliffs that surrounded the building and in the torrent of rain (the torrent of rain was visible), with lightning flashing, a majestic voice said through the sound of the rainfall, *Believe in Jesus Christ and you will be saved!* I stood still and stared. I thought it over and wondered about the experience; then, I quickly returned to the sleeping bag and prayed for help. I asked God to save me from the devils that surrounded me and to get me back home to Iowa.

Such a message I heard in the rain was crucial for my survival. The evil forces were on the verge of overwhelming me to the point of my total destruction. There was no hope. No hope for escape from the evil cult, no hope of finding my way home, no hope of sound mental health. I needed protection and deliverance. I needed God. Desperate, over a course of a few weeks, I was able to procure an airline ticket from reluctant cult leaders, and this began a withdrawal from the horrific experience I had endured for almost four years. The only reason I am alive to tell this story today is because God intervened in my life at the crucial period when I was nearly killed—physically, psychologically, and spiritually. To learn more of my story and the trajectory of my life from this vantage point I refer the reader to my previous series of publications.

*

I now will explain another experience of knowing God, this one peaceful and gentle. I once felt enveloped and immersed within the love and deep peace of God while riding on a city transit bus (a blue one) in a suburb of Iowa City. I was in a wheelchair and my personal care attendant (who previously had been homeless) sat across the aisle from me. After many years of abuse and mistreatment by several female physicians who were bullies, I made a switch and was going to my first appointment with a new male doctor. I was incapable of walking because of spinal conditions and needed to use my wheelchair for mobility. My shoulders and arms were too weak to manually move the chair at this time, so my attendant was helpful.

Now the driver of this bus was no ordinary bus driver. He was tall and large. He was so large his body spilled over his seat. It looked like his seatbelt barely fit. His personality which seemed a bit withdrawn or in a meditative frame of mind, helped him to do an excellent job of driving the bus and he did it well (and quietly) with full confidence.

So I was on this bus with these two men of strong character, both outcasts of sorts: my attendant—a poverty-stricken former homeless person—and the driver, a misfit due to his large stature. We were on our way to the clinic where I would be prescribed life-saving medicines and a new treatment plan for my care. God was with us. It was then that I felt a supernatural force that was so very loving—a strong, but gentle spirit that filled the entire bus. I felt held in the love and comfort of God's hands through the Holy Spirit and I felt the deepest peace possible. I felt totally protected and held safe in God's arms. And I was consciously aware of this at the time: I thought, *God is here! God is with us; I can feel God's loving spirit! I feel totally safe, secure, and cared for.*

\*

> He was despised and rejected by men,
> a man of sorrows and acquainted with grief;
> and as one from whom men hide their faces
> he was despised, and we esteemed him not.
> Isaiah 53:3 ESV

Do we encounter God in this world through the presence of humans? I believe it's possible. Once a cold and starving homeless man sitting on a sidewalk who had been rejected by the whole world looked up to me with big brown eyes that expressed an enormous sadness but also a profound, pure love. I knew that I had encountered the crucified Christ in him. And, later on, with a new relationship this friendship fostered, I observed this person getting down on his knees to pray. He not only prayed for himself, he also said prayers for me. And with the sign of the cross used by Roman Catholics, this person blesses and protects me daily with Christ's protection. He will kiss the Bible and images of a cross or words that are sacred to him. He turns the other cheek when persecuted or bullied. His example of patience and lack of retaliation in the face of mistreatment is an inspiration.

This man is nonviolent, peaceful, and nonaggressive. He treats all women with respect, courtesy, and kindness. He'd rather walk away from an attacker than be violent himself. He is moral and trustworthy. He is tolerant, forgiving, and patient. This is someone many landlords would turn away which is a travesty because he would be by far a perfect tenant and would show more civility than many of those who do pass background checks and are allowed in. This man was imprisoned primarily for *trespassing* because as a homeless person he had nowhere to sleep at night. And he was bullied. Then he chose to violate his parole in order to be jailed again to come in from the freezing sub-zero weather where he would have surely perished within hours. But still, landlords don't see the person. They see words on a report saying something regarding law enforcement. To learn more about this man's extraordinary life please see my publication, *Homeless: The Unbefriended Poor*[1]

---

1. Murphy, *Homeless*.

# Other's Experience of God

WHAT WAS DONE IN the last few hundred years and continues to happen in much of contemporary literature to Anne Hutchinson, needs a rebuke. Not only was she denied legal representation in a court of law in 1637, she has continued to be under or misrepresented in today's world through erroneous historical narrative and scholarly accounts.

Anne Hutchinson was a happily married woman to a devoted husband and mother to fourteen children. As a leader in her New England community, Boston, she attended gatherings when younger women gave birth which was also a time when she would give spiritual guidance. Growing up, her father, an English clergyman, had given her an education both in general knowledge and in the biblical scriptures. She could spar with the quickest male minds over logical analysis of any given text. A deeply religious woman, she told of her experience of God speaking to her directly, telling her that she could be assured of her salvation through belief in Jesus Christ. She need not, then, go through the patriarchal hierarchy of the Puritan church for their interpretations of scripture or to obtain salvation and forgiveness of sins. She, by having her own personal experiential relationship with God could interpret scripture for herself, without a male pastoral mediator. This, she said, was to be true for everyone.

To read my complete creative nonfiction short story on Anne Hutchinson on-line publication, (2017) see: https://hopeforrecovery.com/having-tea-with-anne-hutchinson-justice-four-centuries-later/[1]

*

A friend of mine I've known since middle school shared with me her experience of God:

> "I feel God's love when being kind. Also, when seeing and experiencing kindness and helpfulness. And he [Jesus] said to him, 'You shall love the Lord your God with all your heart, and with all your soul, and with all your mind. This is the great and first commandment. And a second is like it, you shall love your neighbor as yourself.'" (Matt. 22:37–39 RSV) "Let no one seek his own good, but the good of his neighbor." (1 Cor. 10:24 RSV) "And the King will answer them, 'Truly, I say to you, as you did it to one of the least of these my brethren, you did it to me.'" (Matt 25:40 RSV).
>
> "Jesus guides us to help those with their backs against the wall in any way we are able. We [she and her husband] help the elderly and youth in our church and community, volunteer in schools and give monetarily to programs serving marginalized groups and friends. We also receive kind acts from others. All of this brings love to a community and hope for peace."

*

The following essay was written by Myrna that describes how she experiences God or Jesus the Christ (as she puts it):

> "Growing up in a family that attended church three times each week meant that I heard about Jesus from a young age. I learned all the stories of his birth, his inquiring into the synagogue at twelve, choosing the disciples, ministering to the masses, healing the sick and then his betrayal and death. And of course, I

---

1. Murphy, *Having Tea*, para 3.

enjoyed the Easter story and following—his flight into heaven. All this I took for granted—but I'm not sure it changed my behavior.

"Much later, maybe in my early twenties, I began to probe into how Jesus met and responded to people. Finally, I saw the lack of selfishness in him. Rather the total love from his Father God that moved his actions. At that time, I was ready to try for that approach in my dealings. Falling short, I just kept plugging away as I was convinced Love is the answer. And God is Love. And God sent Jesus to show us how to Love. And even though I fall short over and over it is still my belief—that Love is the answer. God is the answer. Jesus, the Christ is my Word to follow. Having this as my motto helps me have contentment. There is less stress, my life feels fulfilled. I am a child of God."

# Religious Claims

BELIEVE IN JESUS CHRIST and you'll be saved!
*Saved from what?*

## SEPARATION FROM GOD

*For there is one God, and there is one mediator between God and men, the man Christ Jesus.* (1Tim 2:5 RSV) This scripture verse is essential to understanding that our connection to the life-giver (God) comes through relationship with Jesus Christ. God is the source of life. Every breath we take is given from God. God has power over life and death. Our heart is beating because God causes it to do so. The energy humans need to function with daily is given by God. When we are cut off from the life source we become spiritually dead. In some fundamental and mysterious way prayers, the word of God through the Holy Bible, and worship (for example, during a religious service) there is a spiritual union and feeding of our souls. To turn our back on God is to turn our back on life, itself. Which leads us to:

## SUICIDE/SELF-DESTRUCTION

Suicide comes in many forms. We can commit career or marriage suicide. We can eat harmful foods and drink harmful drinks, abusing our own bodies, thus, shortening our lifespans. We can commit social suicide by acting out our frustrations in ways contrary to acceptable norms, causing ostracization. We can stand up for our own beliefs politically and be imprisoned. We can overdose on drugs (prescribed or illicit). This list is not exhaustive.

Generally, most suicidal people feel hopeless, without purpose, and find no meaningful reason to live. The physical world offers many pleasures but, ultimately, they fall short. We get used to pleasures and then they no longer satisfy, so the search goes on for something new. Some people think that acquiring more and more wealth will make them happy; or another, newer house. People wander outside the marriage. People travel, thinking this will fulfill them, but then are horrified to find bedbugs in their five-star hotel luxury beds and the housekeeper stole their wallet.

I believe we humans were born with a sinful nature and throughout early years and into adulthood this sinful nature manifests itself in frequent rebellion against our maker (God). The struggle is both internal, in our innermost thoughts and desires and, external, with rebellion against authority figures. Becoming consciously aware of this condition is the first step towards gaining some kind of control over oneself. Reaching the point of acknowledgment of one's own weakness and, therefore, one's dependence on God, takes us closer to maturity. Independence, believing one can survive all by oneself, is self-deceiving. Pride, the greatest of all sinful characteristics, will be the downfall. Humble people know how dependent they are not only on the social group; but also how utterly weak they are without some connection to the life-giving, supernatural spiritual creator of the universe. Rebellion against such a life-giving force—the grace of God—a human cannot and will not survive. God's grace is exemplified by the crucified Christ, the Son of God, who died for our sins, making us right with God. To turn our backs on this precious gift is something to be regretted and the deliberate act or progression of this spiritual suicide it not something that can be fixed without God's intervention.

## DEMONS/DEVIL

You will see little children in Halloween costumes that the parents think are so cute or humorous: devils and demons. Little do they know how dangerous this is, to not take seriously the dark realm. Evil things are not to be taken lightly. Denying that the evil spirits exist will make a person more susceptible to being under their control. I don't believe that terror is something to be joked about. Consider what it's like in your worst nightmare, to be surrounded by and attacked by the demonic. Hear the screams of the demons, the profanities, as they verbally assault you. Tearing at your skin with sharp nails and biting with fierce teeth. Even though you plead with them to stop, it goes on continually in a deep darkness. Being terrified, you run, run, trying to get away, but to no avail. There is no escape.

The supernatural demonic voices I heard were very real, indeed, and carried on for about eighteen months straight before I received assistance. As I was hospitalized in the University of Iowa Psychiatric Hospital and given antipsychotic medication, it helped enormously to be surrounded by good, caring medical professionals. Eventually, the loud voices died down to a murmur. We need *both*: psychiatric medications (given by God to help the brain block out the noise) and the spiritual power of Jesus Christ who has authority over all evil forces in the spiritual realm, who can protect us. *And Jesus came and said to them, "All authority in heaven and on earth has been given to me."* (Matt. 28:18 RSV) Which brings us to the climax of disregarding the love and grace of God lavished upon us during our earthly lifetimes which we might tragically, and flippantly ignore.

## HELL

Hell, according to my understanding, is total (and possibly, eternal) separation from all that is good, true, and beautiful. The beings there don't want to be around each other and try to escape. Violence, turmoil, strife, you name it, anything goes there but peace.

The selfish can now completely have their way unhindered at the cost of the other inhabitants. Profanity, screams, and the writhing of twisted bodies in a never-ending torture of pain and discomfort in flames of fire. Agony, the ugly sound of grinding teeth, anguish, who knows what awaits? We, who said during our lifetimes: *I don't need God. I am smarter. I am independent. Me, myself, and I—that's all I need. I am self-sufficient and will find my own happiness my own way. I know what is best. Wisdom of the traditions? Rubish! Wise men? Fool-hardy. Rules? Laws? Commandments? They are made to be broken! I'm in charge! Nobody's going to tell me what to do! I lived my life my way and that's all that matters. There is nothing more important than sex, money, pleasure, and power. I've had it all, I am the greatest! I am God!*

In the end we will all stand before our Maker, the creator of Heaven and earth, myself included. What will we say then? Trembling and faint, are we going to be speechless? Each one of us will receive what is due: *For we must all appear before the judgment seat of Christ, so that each one may receive good or evil, according to what he has done in the body.* (2 Cor 5:10 RSV)

# II

# Influence of Long-Term Christian Faith on Character Development

# Values/Traits/Purpose in Life

WHEN WE THINK OF Spring break in the US what often comes to mind is unrestrained decadence, self-indulgence, alcohol, and licentiousness with bikini-clad bodies on white, sandy beaches in the southeast corner of the country. Contrast with the plans of sacrificial volunteers on Spring break going on mission trips to Third World countries to feed the poor and starving, and to assist the medically deprived. This contrast is extreme. Yet, it happens every year. The experience of missionaries and mission workers can show us examples of self-denial as they leave behind the homey comforts and pleasures of a life in the middle-or upper-middle-class neighborhoods of our cities.

In most Third World service trips, for example, the mission workers will not find air conditioning and will have to endure stifling heat. They will not find bathrooms with luxurious showers of hot water or modern-day toilets with abundant toilet paper. The work will be unlike anything they've known in the US that carries with it frustrations, trials, and challenging difficulties all willingly endured in their service to other human beings. Such endeavors reveal not only hearts of compassion but individuals who take scripture seriously—Jesus Christ's mandate to serve the least of these:

> "For I was hungry and you gave me food, I was thirsty and you gave me drink, I was a stranger and you welcomed me, I was naked and you clothed me, I was sick and you visited me, I was in prison and you came to me.' Then the righteous will answer him, saying, 'Lord, when did we see you hungry and feed you, or thirsty and give

you drink? And when did we see you a stranger and welcome you, or naked and clothe you? And when did we see you sick or in prison and visit you?' And the King will answer them, 'Truly, I say to you, as you did it to one of the least of these my brothers, you did it to me.'" (Matt 25: 35–40 ESV)

The following is the recounting of Becka Simpson's (real name) trip with a mission group affiliated with The Presbyterian Church (USA) in 2002. She currently is a retired social worker. The group went to the small country of Haiti which is the poorest country in the Western Hemisphere, Latin America, and Caribbean (LAC). What are the character traits, values, and motivations of someone who would volunteer for such an endeavor? This short narrative is provided to give a glimpse into such traits such as altruism, courage, compassion, and kindness. These traits are exemplified as those within the character of one who is often affiliated with a Christian religious community. It was my honor to interview Becka. Here is Becka's story:

"I went to Haiti with a church high school group, including two of my daughters. My oldest daughter had already gone to Haiti and she loved it, so I knew it was something I wanted to experience for myself. It would be at the Central Plateau of Haiti and I wanted to see what it was like."

What did the group want to accomplish? What were their goals?

"It was two-fold. There were some people with a medical background so there were some medical clinic days planned. There was an eye doctor who came and he had brought a lot of eye glasses, so they had an eye clinic planned. And there were also some physical needs like painting and cleaning for the school there, preparing classrooms for use."

What were the living conditions for you and the people in the area where you worked?

"This was my first experience in a Third World country. We slept in bunk beds, a type of barracks, with ten beds to a room. At night we could hear either rats or mice going along the rafters.

## Values/Traits/Purpose in Life

There was an outhouse and you had to be careful that there weren't scorpions or spiders. The shower was heated by the sun, they had a big water tank. So, it was pretty primitive. They had a filtration system for our drinking water, so you could bring your water bottle and fill it.

"As for the Haitian people, I never saw anyone without clothing; but perhaps some of them didn't have shoes. The outdoor temperatures were usually in the 80s. What I do remember clearly is that the roads were really bad. There were no paved roads; it was all dirt. If it rained, there would be these big potholes. What made a big impression on me was that before every outing the missionaries would gather and pray over the truck, that the vehicle would hold up, that the tires would hold up, and that the roads would be sufficiently passable—that there would not be an incident. This was all a big deal. They had vehicles that weren't new and we were worried about a mechanical failure. So this was eye opening."

Did you ever feel in danger?

"Our group did not feel concerned about being assaulted by rebels or dangerous people. There was some talk about voodoo. But I never experienced anything dangerous. We were on the plateau, in the heart of Haiti, and away from the main cities. We did have guards patrolling the compound every night, but I always felt safe. Since the compound was gated and they had someone patrol the area at night I know that they recognized that there could be danger." [Author's interjection: During December 2001 and the years that closely followed, Haiti underwent great upheaval with an attempted coup, and rebels' violent and often fatal attacks on government officials, and some civilians. There was general unrest and dangerous conditions throughout certain parts of the country, but not all.][1]

Did you converse with the people there?

"I could not speak their language, so did not have conversations with them. My group was there through a weekend and I went to a church service. The Haitian people, generally speaking, seemed happy. There was a lot of singing and laughter. The women

1. Norton, "Coup Attempt," 4.

who prepared meals for us were lovely. I worked in a school building to prepare it for classes and also worked in the eye clinic. One of my tasks was to dispense medication and what we had were things like aspirin or anti-acid tablets, things like that. These were not drugs that you needed a prescription for."

What about their physical condition?

"I didn't see people who were emaciated. There were some women who looked pretty fit. You walked everywhere; there were very few cars. So you did a lot of walking. Some people were a little overweight probably because their meals had more starches. For our meals the missionaries were served chicken, rice, and beans a lot. They had wonderful peanut butter and wonderful coffee. There was also bread, eggs, and sugar. A lot of chickens running around!"

What was something important you learned during your trip that really stood out?

"I learned so much about the world by going on that trip. People can talk about a Third World country, but until I could see it, I didn't really understand it. And that was really helpful. It forced me to be more generous in my giving; to recognize that everything we have is a gift from God. It's not our abilities; it's God's gift. There are many ways to recognize that but I'm not sure I would have recognized it without a missionary experience. My take on experiencing Haiti is that I saw that we can live with so much less. It didn't make me decide to give everything away and live a monastic life, but opened me up to that possibility. I am reminded of the *eye of the needle* parable of Jesus. [Again, I tell you, it is easier for a camel to go through the eye of a needle than for a rich person to enter the kingdom of God. (Matt 19:24 ESV)]" [End of Becka Simpson part].

\*

A friend of mine chose to become a social worker as a young adult and I asked her if it was her Christian faith and beliefs that led her to become a social worker, a profession aiming to help others? I asked: "Is there a connection?"

She said: "Jesus›s example over and over was about social justice and helping the least of these and those with their backs against the wall. So, *yes*, to your question."

\*

Cecilia Norris, MD, spent some time in Guatemala serving as a medical missionary. The following information gives us some insight into what motivates a person to do such demanding work and how character development influences the life choices we make. I first asked her: What motivated you to go to Guatemala when there is so much danger in the developing nations?

"My parents had an influence on me in serving others both in my community and abroad. They were active in social justice issues and included their kids in volunteer opportunities whenever they could. I have memories of taking wallpaper off of walls for houses that were being renovated for families in need.

"Some of my motivation also likely came from a trip I took to the Philippines. I had wanted to do mission work for a long time. I went to the Philippines during high school and saw the people there who were living and working in much more challenging conditions than I had ever experienced; however, it took many years after that trip before I had the opportunity to go with a church group to Guatemala."

What is it in your background that gave you the courage to risk your life to serve there?

"It can be hard to determine the actual risks of going to a foreign country. There are risks of violence, accidents, illness. However, many of those risks exist here in the United States as well. When my family was going to Guatemala (as volunteers), my husband looked up the murder rate and found that it was lower than the murder rate in Saint Louis in the 90's when we both worked in North Saint Louis and lived close to a neighborhood where it was not uncommon to hear gun shots. In addition, the Impacto team [a program in Guatemala], since they live in the country, are very aware of when political unrest or COVID or travel restrictions can impact the safety of visiting teams. When we needed to spend a night in Guatemala City we were always in a locked community. I was not concerned for my personal safety. There is still theft to be concerned about, especially in the tourist cities, but it was similar risk [I had on my trip] to Spain. I was warned about the bus rides down the mountains on curvy roads in Guatemala. When we first started going on mission trips there, I was much more nervous. We were stopped by a rockslide on one trip, but since then the roads have been improved. The bus drivers are very skilled but, yes, an accident is always a concern.

"I am a very privileged person, so from that perspective this may have been considered a dangerous trip because I was getting away from the things that gave me personal comfort. But my children, friends, reading, and prayers have taught me to recognize that privilege for what it is. I was much less in danger traveling to Guatemala than the people who live there or even under-resourced people in the US. In my prayer and discernment time I did feel confident that this mission trip would bring me closer to God."

Did you hear a calling from God to go there? Once, or several times?

"I think I did hear callings but they were different every time I have gone. The first trip seemed more like an adventure with two of my children and church friends. I was caught up in the excitement of planning, of finally doing, if only for a week, what I had thought I would do as a calling way back in high school. Participating on short term mission trips is different than being a full-time missionary. I am sure that God put me where I needed to be at the time I needed to be there."

Can you describe this experience?

"There have been many experiences. After the first trip, I felt called to return. I was able to see how the partnership that Saint Andrew has with Impacto Ministries in Guatemala is valuable for all participants as well as for the people we serve. Since Impacto staff live in the communities and have developed relationships with individuals they are able to see the needs first hand. They can then guide us in the best way to serve. In preparation for our trips, we tried to understand how to *help without hurting."*

What were your duties there? What did you do there?

"All the trips are only a week long and with travel and rest time, they can range from five to six days of truly serving. Saint Andrew tries to see what the greatest needs are. Since I am a physician, I have been frequently asked to do medical clinics. My family medicine provided me the basic scientific and medical training but the actual living conditions and resources in Guatemala impact people's health more than in the US. We found that doing relatively simple things like giving people vitamins or applying fluoride to teeth, dispensing anti-parasite medicines, listening to their stories, playing with them, and sharing food with them improved their well-being the most. The Impacto program has many different ministries that I have been able to participate in in a very minor role over the past eight years—Happy Tummies (feeding children lunch and teaching), Abuelitos (feeding the elderly and giving them a safe place to rest), construction projects (helped build a house for a family and worked on Happy Tummies wall), and Sports camp. Other people from our group participated in the other projects more than I did, including some that I did not help with."

What were the living conditions for you there and those of the natives?

"The living conditions for our group were really very nice. It felt more like a vacation because other people cooked for us and cleaned our rooms. We stayed in very nice complexes with multiple rooms and multiple beds per room. The Promised Land and Hillside buildings were/are safe, clean, and comfortable. There was not the best hot water on our earlier trips and we needed to be sure to not drink untreated water or street food. The hardest thing for me to remember was to not dispose of toilet paper in the toilets. The plumbing throughout Guatemala cannot handle it. It was hard to see the trash in the fields and the sides of the roads because they do not have easy city disposal like we do here; but I noticed an improvement of that over the past eight years.

"The living conditions for Guatemalans were varied. The poverty is greater than in the US, but there are many people who live very well there. The Happy Tummies children frequently go home to places without running water or electricity. Heat and cooking are done by wood-burning so we saw a lot of respiratory symptoms. Without sanitation, parasites were common as well. However, the homes that we visited as part of our home visits, were usually very clean (dirt floors swept to a shine) and the people were very welcoming and wanted to share what they could."

How did you survive this experience?

"It was not difficult. If was extremely rewarding and I really never felt in danger."

What were your rewards or what did you gain?

"I gained friendships, understanding of other people's struggles and joys. It does make me appreciate even more the many luxuries I have in the US."

What is some of the wisdom you gained from your experience?

"I learned that if we are open to learning from other people's life experiences, beliefs, and behaviors, we can better minister to them as Jesus showed us how to do."[End of Norris part]

*

Another example of the influence of religious faith on personality development or how faith in God influences cognitive, emotional, and behavioral outcomes, is the following: I interviewed a person (who wishes to remain anonymous) about the volunteer missionary work the person did in Indonesia:

"I grew up in a church and went on my first mission trip as a teenager which gave me a heart for serving other people. As an adult and while I was living in Colorado, I had a car accident. After walking away without a scratch, I thought: why was I spared? Very close to this time I found out that two other people had had accidents also; but they were both seriously injured. I thought, maybe I need to do something with my life to serve God and to benefit other human beings. I then became motivated to do mission work in Indonesia for a span of time. I went to Indonesia with a group. I had been working as a physical therapist previously for four years. I took a break from that and received training. The group I was in did short term ministry work in Indonesia for about six weeks. Our role in Indonesia was to support the long-term missionaries. I did not go as a physical therapist, but was able to use some of my skills when called upon while there. For example, once a male missionary got injured and I was the medical support person there. We could not drink the water and used bottled water. And we could not eat the street food; but we could eat what our hosts cooked in their homes. We stayed in modest, small motel-like structures or in private homes.

"As for things I learned: Sometimes we lose sight of God's presence in our lives, when surrounded by so much. I also learned that there is a much bigger world than what I had previously been aware of. That God is everywhere. We have a lot of things here in the US that we take for granted; and people in other countries are able to survive on much less." [End of Indonesia part]

*

Another example of the influence of religious faith on personality development or how faith in God influences cognitive, emotional, and behavioral outcomes is the following: A married couple who are Christian medical missionaries by the names of Dr(s) Lynn and Sharon Fogleman have made numerous trips to Africa (as well as other locations) to serve some of the poorest people in the world. The striking thing about this is that they are putting their lives at risk. During Autumn 2024, as I write this, Uganda, one country in the area they work in, has had some violence and there have been attacks on Christian people by extremists, with attacks not only against their own locals, but also the foreign Christan workers that come to aid them. The Foglemans give up the comforts of their own home in the Midwestern United States to go for a period of time to South Sudan, Uganda, and Kenya, and other locations where there is no air conditioning. Temperatures in South Sudan are sometimes above one hundred-ten degrees F.

I did an interview with the Foglemans which is as follows:

Marcia: I'm interested in the work you did in Africa. You mentioned that you were in several different countries. Could you please describe the countries?

Dr. Lynn Fogleman: Yes, we've been in several countries in Africa, both east and west. We've spent most of our time in Kenya. We lived there for ten years. And we've lived in and worked in some other African countries.

Dr. Sharon Fogleman: After our children finished high school, then we felt God was calling us to go to another place in Africa. We found people who were serving in South Sudan, so we decided to join them. We went for a visit and found that there was definitely some public health education that was necessary. There were a lot of villages that needed help just learning some basics for how to stay healthy. And so we were there for four and a half years until the war came, and then we left and went to Uganda.

Marcia: What motivated you to do this type of work? What inspired you to do work in the developing nations?

Dr. Lynne Fogleman: As I became a follower of Jesus, I wanted to let my life to be able to show his love in a way that brought me into contact with people in their deepest need. And that's actually, one of main reasons I felt compelled to go to medical school. But even though I was in medical school, I wasn't actually thinking about missions at that time. But during a Bible study that I was attending during my time in medical school, one of the senior students came and gave a presentation on his short-term trip to the Dominican Republic.

I'd never even considered missions before then. He was a senior student; I'm not sure I ever saw him again after that presentation because he was very busy in his clinical years and didn't get to attend the Bible study very often. I was a junior student and I thought maybe that was something I might like to do someday. And I ended up going on a short-term, two-week trip to the Dominican Republic. And it was while I was there that I really think

God called me into missions. I saw the receptiveness of the people both to the treatment that we were giving and to the Gospel message. They were people who did not have much previous medical care, were very appreciative and interactive; and were also open to hearing the Gospel, and discussions of faith [we used translators]. As I left that two-week experience during which I met Sharon, also, for the first time, as I left that and went back to medical school and into the technological, and rapid-pace medicine world of the US, I was moved in many, many ways to believe that working with people in developing countries was not only reaching people who had much more need in terms of availability of medical care; and also had great need for hearing the world of God and the Gospel of Jesus Christ. And as I found that that experience was so rewarding and also so needed I thought as I spoke with God, I thought, *You know, Lord, this really seems like it could be something that I could really, really feel passionate about doing.* And he kept that fire burning in my heart throughout the rest of medical school, throughout my three years of residency, throughout two years of service I owed to the state of Kansas for paying my tuition for medical school. All of those years I began to realize that this is what I was called to do.

Marcia, to Sharon: What is it in your background that gave you the heart to do this type of work?

Dr. Sharon Fogleman: It's a process. I had had an understanding that missionaries were just pushing the Gospel and that people weren't actually understanding it because we were not doing it well. So as I was going through med school I met people who were mission-minded and that's what motivated me to continue to see what it's like. There were people I knew at Saint Andrew [the church she attends] through choir and other things, and that's how I began to think that sharing the love of Jesus is what I can do. And Lynn and I had met each other but we were both in training; we did not have a lot of understanding, I didn't speak Spanish, so I needed the interpreters. Just being able to see how people could love one another in the midst of no language similarity, but also I learned that they were reception to what we had to say. And we got to know like-minded people, people from Michigan and from all kinds of places. And we could see that God can use that even if it's not exactly what you imagine the missionary would be.

So, I definitely was taken to church throughout my life and yet I kept learning what it was like to love someone that you were just getting to meet and how you could help them. That was a part of the transition of medical student, going to residency, getting to know people who are very different but recognizing we can still love each other and learn and grow when we don't even know for sure what we are doing. I learned a lot from watching other mission people and watching how doctors can definitely share that experience and someone is blessed. And usually it's both people who are blessed. You learn that you don't need a lot of things to live and to grow.

Marcia: What were some of your duties there?

Dr. Lynn Fogleman: Our duties varied because we were in different countries doing different things and that remains even to this day. In our ten years in Kenya, our duties were primarily around the mission hospital where we worked. We would make rounds on seeing patients on our assigned wards; and if a patient needed a procedure, we would do that procedure. I happened to be on maternity for much of that time in Kenya and ended up doing many C-sections and obstetric procedures for women who were pregnant or in labor. Also being on call at night to see patients with any problem. And then in our latter years I was selected to be the medical superintendent of the hospital. And therefore my life changed greatly because although I still did my share of night call and weekend call to help out in the doctoring duties, I was doing a lot of administration representing the hospital at different meetings, chairing the heads of departments, oversaw all the works of the hospital. So, it was very different duty at that time. Then we went from Kenya to serve in mission in southwest Kentucky to serve the people in Appalachia for fourteen years. We saw patients in a clinic. And then when we went to South Sudan we did more community education on disease prevention and community health. And then when we went to Uganda, I was back doing C-sections on a maternity ward. And since that time we live in the

## Values/Traits/Purpose in Life

US but still make frequent trips to various countries and have done things like trauma healing trainings/sessions so that other people can help care for the emotional trauma of their friends and family and other people that they know. We have mentored medical students, nursing students who are contemplating the possibility of serving long-term missions overseas.

Marcia: Was there something in your past history that gave you a heart to serve others in medical missions?

Dr. Lynn Fogleman: I was brought up in a church and my father was the pastor. As a college student I was living a rather superficial and unsatisfying life without meaning or purpose. But when I dedicated my life to Jesus, things changed dramatically. As a part of following Jesus, serving other human beings with love and care is what Jesus taught, so I wanted to do that.

Dr. Sharon Fogleman: We had three young children while in Kenya, so I was at home more and we had two Kenyan women who helped with childcare, housework, and cooking. The children went to the local school and learned some of the language and they had wonderful friends. It was a nice environment for them, it was a rural area and they loved it.

Marcia: What were some of the challenges there? Maybe, was it the climate? Did it get really hot there in Africa?

Dr. Lynn Fogleman: The hottest place we ever served was in South Sudan. Indeed, we did not have air conditioning there, but we used fans. We used battery powered bedside fans close to each of our heads at night so that we could sleep. Yes, during the day there, whilst walking—we would be sweating quite a lot. And we never went anywhere without taking water with us. Temperatures there probably got up to over 110 degrees F at the hottest time of the day, during the hottest months of the year. We were so glad that we lived in the hills of Kenya (at 6,000 feet elevation) during our ten years of working in the mission hospital there—and raising the kids. Temperatures were much better there. There were even some cool times of the year there due to the elevation.

Marcia: What were some of the rewards you gained from doing this work?

## Concerning the Importance of God for Mental Health

Dr. Lynn Fogleman: First and foremost, knowing that I was serving Jesus seeking to follow the call that he had placed on my heart. That serving him and seeking to do the best I could do and that as we as a family would be the greatest reward. That's the main reason we went there, that would be the main reason we did this work was to serve him and follow his call. So that's rewarding when you know you are walking with him simply to do your best to serve. But blessings go very much both ways: to serve in different cultures than our own, get to see people of another culture, to befriend and get to know them. To see that there are different people in this world with a different worldview, who have a different understanding of things; we can learn from them. It was rewarding to be challenged in our faith, stretched in our faith, medically, professionally, but just personally through an experience that takes you out of your comfort zone. And although it was not always comfortable, as you look back at your life you see what a blessing it really was.

Marcia: What was some wisdom you learned while working there.

Dr. Lynn Fogleman: I will tell you a short story: I had to go out to a local person's home to say something or deliver a message and as I was leaving, she asked: "Can you share a cup of tea with us?"

I said, "No, I'm sorry, there are many things I need to do at the hospital (which was true)."

She said, "You mean you don't have time to stop and share a cup of tea with us?"

I realized that stopping to talk and get to know the hearts and lives of people is more important that accomplishing a list of items on a busy to-do list. So I did stay for a while with this family and had a cup of tea with them and got to know them. They taught me the importance of learning about the lives of people, getting to know them. I found this is what really matters. So family is very important and community.

Marcia: Sharon, what are some things you learned by doing this mission work?

## Values/Traits/Purpose in Life

Dr. Sharon Fogleman: He mentioned the community aspect. And we learned the importance of that because no one can really survive or make it on their own. Especially when it comes to caring for people who are very poor, who have very little for food, people help them out. And we learned that if you are in a community, it requires that you be respectful and you look at things with different eyes. We don't have to have all these items and things that make us look better, like more toys for children. You don't need much to survive. But if you are in a community that is open to helping others, then you soon learn that this is what life is really about. You don't have to have a lot of personal items; but if you can share with other people, then that is a positive way to be part of community. In general, it was a rich experience. It was hard, many times, very hard. The work was difficult for Lynn and I because we stood for long periods, especially when doing surgery and when making rounds on the wards. During periods, outbreaks of malaria and measles, it was emotionally difficult because so many children died. Spiritually it was challenging, especially when the weeks kept us very busy. But our Kenyan and international colleagues provided a lot of support and fellowship as well. I worked on children's ward primarily. Children are very fragile when they're young. Many died of malaria, pneumonia, and measles. And we didn't see that here in the states, that was rare. But we were able to interact with the parents, come to know them and see their challenges. And that was so meaningful for all of us.

Dr. Sharon Fogleman continues: You can be in Kenya, you can be in Nicaragua, you can be in so many places; yet, just watching and seeing how people live a rich life even though they don't have a lot of physical things, they still live a rich life and often they appear happier than those who live in the states or in Western countries. And so it's a fascinating part about living among others. That is one of the richest parts of it.

Dr. Lynn Fogleman: That is such an important point; I would like to add a little bit more. People often ask us about going back, or if you've spent your life in missions, going back, many, many times to places that are not as developed as the West. People ask:

## Concerning the Importance of God for Mental Health

*Why? Why would you do it?* I feel that not only is it in service to the Lord; but you really feel drawn to go back. And people would think: *Well, what is it that draws you to go back where it's hard or there aren't as many things. There's some risk of illness? What is it that draws you to go back?* I say: it's really the people who come out of an experience of life that shows the importance of a relationship with God, with one another—and they know how to enjoy them. Because they know that life if short. And they expect for life to be short. Whereas we in the West labor and expect life to be long, to enjoy things, and experiences. I think we are drawn to the people in Africa, we are in awe and in wonder to see how these people love and laugh, and express joy, and enjoy one another in ways we don't see here very much in the US, the West. I think they see what is important in life more clearly, maybe than we do. [End of Foglemans' part]

\*

In counterpoint to the example of the service of missionaries I would imagine a person being focused solely on him or herself, all the while seeking power and dominance over others; someone who exploits the weak, whose aim is status, wealth, and the accumulation of goods for no other reason but the feeling of possessing; one who seeks pleasure at the cost of others through exploitation; who has a hedonistic lifestyle with comfort as top priority. In this scenario the only affection for others is that which is self-serving. As a friend said in a Bible study years ago: S-I-N, the "I" is in the center and shows a lack of respect for the dignity and value of human life. People who are self-serving are also more likely to be angry people, short-tempered, and impatient who are often loud with profuse use of obscenities.

Along with making physical sacrifices missionaries usually exhibit certain psychological or emotional strengths. These would be exhibiting compassion, patience, kindness, and endurance. The ability to cope with frustration is another common characteristic of this group. Acceptance of differences, especially different races

## Values/Traits/Purpose in Life

or ethnic groups, and tolerance of cultural tastes is evident. What stands out is the most important thing of all: love of God and other people, especially as they encounter the poor and sick in their work—sharing the love of Christ.

In order to do missionary work a strong mental health is required. These people usually have an emotional and intellectual constitution out of the ordinary. Backbone or strong character would be a prerequisite to withstand both, the physical and mental hardships encountered in the course of their work. Many do not come away unscathed. There are or can be injuries of both body and soul. Endurance and perseverance are strongly required to do this type of work.

*

I studied situational or social factors involved that strengthen mental health, along with the spiritual and work-related outcomes. For Patti, it was having religion as a part of her life from a young age. From four through six, she attended a Presbyterian Sunday school. It was her first experience with other children. She liked the stories and the Christmas pageant. She can still remember the names of two of the girls in the class.

When Patti answered the question of what person had a big impact upon her life she said that several school teachers fit this: the vocal teacher for her high school choir and a private piano teacher who remains as a friend to this day. Patti grew up in a small town in a school where she could be a part of most activities and she had three younger brothers. Her grandmother said she thought Patti would be a nurse. And this became reality. Patti believes that having God as a part of her life during her high school years was very important and, also as an adult she is a member of a congregation which is an important part of her life of faith. [End of Patti's part]

## Concerning the Importance of God for Mental Health

\*

As a survivor of psychosis, PTSD, clinical depression, and, unfortunately—extreme poverty, I will now touch upon what aspect of my spiritual life has been the most important to me in my recovery process which led to transformation of my life and personal character. What has been helpful in my life of faith, as well as least helpful or at worst, destructive? I build upon the following terms to help others become aware of the blessings and, at times, roadblocks, that I have encountered during a recovery process from mental illness. This touches upon formation of a person's cognitive, emotional, and behavioral development.

The list of terms below could be used in a therapeutic setting with the doctor/counselor bringing up the topics to discuss with the patient: *What do you think of this term?* [provides written or spoken term] *What comes to mind? Does it prompt any emotions or thoughts? Please share what you are comfortable with and we can discuss it.*

This type of activity is an exercise in reflection. Discovering significant aspects of the patient's life in the course of introspection could be instrumental in furthering the recovery process. These reflections could assist the patient in finding real meaning for their lives. I quote Chris C.H. Cook: *If we really believe that meaning is important to patients, it needs to be seen as important by psychiatrists too. The concerns of psychiatry (psychopathology, diagnosis, psychotherapy and so on) need to be more, not less, entangled with the concerns of the human subject as patient. This does not mean that the boundaries of good professional practice should be thrown to the wind. It does mean that psychiatry needs to be more meaningful—in a compassionate and patient-centered understanding of itself as deeply entangled with the wider human quest for meaning.*[2]

Before I get to the list of words, I will mention that it is quite obvious and goes without saying that if a person lacks food, clothing, and shelter, they cannot survive and so identifying meaning (other than survival) takes a back seat. Granted, my parents

---

2. Cook, *Hearing Spiritual Voices*, 120.

## Values/Traits/Purpose in Life

provided these physical things as I grew up and I'm grateful. Upon adulthood, as I left the cult, it was the provisions of mental health professionals who took me in. They provided government benefits for a very sick human being. I was not well enough to apply for benefits myself, the SSI (Supplemental Security Income) and Medicaid. I did get placed in a women's psychiatric patients' half-way house when discharged from the psychiatric hospital. That lasted only a few months because of social conflict within the house. I tried various means of employment but was too emotionally sick to do it. I was aided in finding an apartment along with being provided the government's financial Housing Assistance. My social isolation caused me to look for friendship and companionship but I only found destructive relationships with emotionally and physically violent men who appeared to lack a conscience. Sometimes, because of poverty, I lacked adequate clothing, especially during the harsh winter months. Buying enough food was also a challenge. To sum up this category: food, clothing, and shelter, I barely scraped by, I barely survived. During my early to mid-adult years, I tried to attend worship services at churches, but usually lacked transportation. The Christians did not take an interest in me or my welfare. I was clearly an outsider. The church people were the insiders; I was outside of the Christian social groups.

So here are some terms below to offer a patient for them to reflect on. I provide some of my own thoughts:

## SAFETY/SECURITY

I know some mentally ill people who are homeless and live, daily, without security or safety. This must be very difficult for them. As a young adult, there came into my life a psychiatrist who spent extra time with me therapeutically which gave me some stability. I knew he was one person I could count on. I did not find security from my relationships with relatives which were in a constant state of friction and strife. When there was not one friend I could count on, this caused anxiety. However, when my psychiatrist took the time to help me by listening to my concerns this made all the difference and I felt some degree of periodic safety and was then able to eventually form some friendships.

We would expect to find some degree of safety in God's house, a church; but this is not always the case. Granted, most churchgoers try to be loving and kind. However, gossip, backstabbing, and tones of voice that stab and bite does exist among a few people. Sometimes, it feels like warfare. It seems that bullies exist even in God's house. For some reason which God has chosen not to reveal to me personally, there can be cruel words exchanged and usually without warrant.

I don't always feel peace at church. Sometimes, I'm tense and on the defense, actually, hypervigilant. People are promoting various ideologies, sides are taken, there are numerous camps and competitions. Power struggles, which Jesus said have no place in God's kingdom, still exist in his house on earth. When people forget about a servant's heart and instead try to obtain dominance over others, this runs contrary to Christ's teaching. As things stand right now, I will try to protect myself. Which leads us to the next term:

## ACCEPTANCE

Where do we find acceptance? Where can we go? Are we doomed to social strife? I find there are a few individuals who treat me with kindness on a regular basis. My closest friend, a middle-age man, is the gentlest, most humble, and loving person I know. His manner toward me is consistently kind, protective, and caring. I also feel accepted by some female friends, one is a physician by profession, and the other, someone I knew in middle school, currently a retired social worker. There are others. You are probably wondering why I don't list any of my biological family members. That just didn't happen in my lifetime. Maybe beyond the grave Heaven may hold some answers.

## ACCOUNTABILITY

I try to be accountable and keep my promises. I try to keep my word. If I say I'm going to do something, I try to do it. If people can't count on me, that's a bad thing. Our reputation is at stake: are we known as a liar, someone who won't keep their word? Or someone who is responsible and trustworthy? Keeping your word shows integrity. I strive to improve on this.

## REPENTANCE

Failing to live by God's standards on many occasions I find the need to repent before God for these shortcomings. When not repenting, the weight upon my conscience and shoulders becomes nearly unbearable. I believe a lot of depression among the mentally ill is the result of not saying, "I'm sorry," to God or being made right with God. If we confess our sins, God, in his mercy, forgives, and we are made clean. Being made clean, there is a lightness in our heart.

## BLESSING

We receive blessings and we can also be a blessing for others.

## CENTEREDNESS

There's self-centeredness which is generally frowned upon, while looking beyond the self to a higher power, purpose, activity, or goal is a healthier direction.

## CLARITY

Mental fog is a term frequently used these days to denote a lack of direction, purpose, and vision. It helps to read literature that points to what I need to do with my day. Finding books or articles in libraries or on-line is helpful. Step by step suggestions help me to organize my activities while leaving room for creativity. Some people don't believe that they are creative. I don't know the reason for this. Fear of the unknown? Or maybe, a lack of abstraction in thinking? Is creativity considered abstract thought? At any rate, I've experienced large periods in my life history when I called myself *Marcia the Marshmallow*. This is because I felt soft, mushy and without backbone. I lacked an internal locus of control with which to be motivated. Finding the strength within ourselves that directs our every day lives promotes action, both mental and physical. This is intrinsic. Extrinsic motivation won't last because some day the external will be gone. Having something within ourselves is what lasts, reflective of our character.

## COMMITMENT

Being committed or committing ourselves to some thought, idea, person, or thing is helpful. Going out, uncontrolled, in all directions is the wide road; but focusing on what we want to do and work on until it is completed, is better. Societal norms reward commitment while infidelity is frowned on. Loyalty to people, ideas, and/or institutions even when it is difficult is a worthy goal.

## COMPASSION

We've all experienced first-hand mistreatment and abuse from others at one time or another so it is obvious to us that we would prefer compassion from others. Doing unto others the way we, ourselves, want to be treated is the well-known saying. How we learn to be compassionate is a topic addressed in a previous publication, see *The Compassionate Psychiatrist: Redefining Mental Healthcare*.[3]

The following list of words are, additionally, food for thought and possible subjects for psychotherapeutic exploration for the

3. Murphy, *Compassionate Psychiatrist*, 16–20.

## VALUES/TRAITS/PURPOSE IN LIFE

purpose of developing a patient's cognitive, emotional, and behavioral outcomes: *Courage, Discipline, Faith, Forgiveness, Gratitude, Healing, Hope, Joy, Kindness, Love, Meaning, Patience, Purpose, Serenity, Trust, Understanding, Vision, Wisdom.*

# Daily Life

## When Faith Makes a Difference

WHAT ARE THE IMPLICATIONS of having religious beliefs? Will religious beliefs have an impact on our daily lives? How will religious beliefs influence our values? I know that each spiritual person is different in what they might value the most as they carry out actions in their everyday lives. I did a survey (albeit non-scientific) amongst a group of church attendees to see what their priorities were and what was on their mind; and in what ways do they direct their daily activities. I summarized the results according to the most important to the less important. Of course there will be different opinions amongst individuals all across the world; this is just a glimpse of a segment of a church-going population in the Midwest US. The findings are helpful to show how a religious faith can lead to a healthy lifestyle. The results suggest ways that psychiatric patients would benefit from becoming involved in a religious community and using daily spiritual exercises (practices). The top three items listed as the most important to these participants were: marriage, parenting, and spiritual life. Coming in second was friends/social life, work, education/training, and physical self-care. Next came: citizenship/community life and recreation/fun.

In addition, I asked a group of Christian church-attendees if they were usually completely bored/exuberant, enthusiastic, or does it fluctuate? The majority said: exuberant and enthusiastic, and some said it fluctuates. Most said that life seems to be a mixture of the routine with some excitement also. All of the people in the survey said that they have very clear goals and aims; and that their personal existence is very purposeful and meaningful. Everyday life varies between the same things going on with something new and different. In achieving life goals, they have made progress and some have reached complete fulfillment. Most responded that their lives are running over with exciting good things. They said that if they should die today that they would feel that their life has been very worthwhile. In thinking about their lives most responded that they always see a reason for their being here and when viewing the world in relation to their lives, the world, for some, fit meaningfully with their life; while some answered that sometimes, it seems a bit challenging to understand this. All of the respondents answered that they see themselves as very responsible people. The majority believed that concerning freedom to make one's own choices, that a person is both, limited somewhat by heredity and environment, as well as able to make some of our life choices freely.

Regarding death, most of the participants in the survey said that they are prepared and unafraid, while some said it was not so clear cut. Regarding suicide, most have not considered it an option, with only one who mentioned it did cross their mind occasionally. All the participants said that regarding their ability to find a meaning, purpose, or mission in life, this was very great. Many respondents answered that they felt their life was in God's hands. They also felt that facing their daily tasks is a source of pleasure and satisfaction; that they have discovered in the course of their life-times clear-cut goals, and a satisfying life purpose.

# III

Partners/Therapeutic Process

# Religious Pluralism and Therapy

FAILURE TO SEEK OR take steps towards recovery results in darkness and possibly, destruction. As I've mentioned in earlier chapters an individual's day to day focus will determine the outcome of their lives. Playing video games 24/7 will amount to nothing. People need people and, ultimately, God. As a Christian I believe that we come to know God through Jesus Christ, his Son.

Different worldviews/beliefs of therapists and patients makes Religiously-Integrated Cognitive Behavioral Therapy (RCBT) impossible to be effective. A therapist cannot maintain personal integrity if they say to the patient that they support other religions than what they themselves actually and, truly, believe in. On the other hand: *Proselytizing for atheism or agnosticism is no less a professional ethical concern than proselytizing for a particular religious stance.*[1] Not only non-belief in a higher power can come across during the therapy session from the counselor and/or patient; but belief in a particular religious stance can become apparent. Things get very murky because we are dealing with various perspectives from different people who are trying to communicate. How can the therapist retain their mental integrity?

I am not a professor nor a psychiatric professional. I am a mental patient with cognitive deficits which have an impact upon my intellectual processes and impede my comprehension. My interests are also difficult to maintain over long periods of time. Even

1. Cook, *Hearing Spiritual Voices*, 104.

so, I do have a few thoughts on the matter of pluralism in the field of medicine and, specifically, psychiatry which follows.

There are some in academia who insult conservative Christians, those with fundamental beliefs in Jesus Christ. Fundamentalist, in this case, is a term used by some in academia in a derogatory manner, often accusatory against those who do not have a pluralistic view of religion. This is not good. I would refer the reader to the book, *The Nicene Creed: An Introduction* by Phillip Cary.[2] This creed is used by millions of ordinary believers in the Christian faith across the globe. Any believer in Christ (of broad definition) who uses the Nicene Creed which summarizes what the Bible teaches about the Holy Trinity and what the Gospel is, is, technically, a fundamentalist, solely because they believe in the fundamental or basic truths on which the Christian faith is based. Criticizing such believers and looking down on them is a criticism of the Christian faith itself. When such believers are accused of being bigoted and narrow minded because they reject pluralism I would have to say, well, *you* (pluralists) are doing the exact same thing i.e., saying that *only religious pluralism is true and nothing else*. The pluralist person is just as "narrow minded" by saying only their way is the true way, *the pluralistic way*. The same goes for the atheist and agnostic. What we need to do is get beyond the name-calling and accusations and just acknowledge that people have different points of view. Even so, Phil Cary states that the religious pluralism in today's post-modern institutions is a form of modern Western intellectual imperialism.[3]

When medical and psychiatric training calls on the trainee to *show respect* to the other religions this is not worded correctly because the term *respect* implies something of value is being elevated. Instead, it is best to say that a person can abide by their conscience by emphatically refusing to deny Christ by stating that all religions are equally true; but they are free to respect *the people (human beings)* of different faiths. Various faith traditions which differ from Christianity cannot logically co-exist with Christianity. Therefore,

---

2. Cary, *Nicene Creed*.
3. Murphy, *Knitting Barbed Wire*, 25.

I will only respect something that I believe is true, not false. So the emphasis must be upon respecting the *human beings* who hold different theological viewpoints while keeping one's loyalty to one's own theological beliefs. This is the only way to keep one's intellectual integrity. *I tell you, on the day of judgment men will render account for every careless word they utter; for by your words you will be justified, and by your words you will be condemned.* (Matt. 12:36–37 RSV)

As far as the psychiatrist providing spiritual guidance, I would say that not all psychiatrists will be comfortable doing this. When one is not then they can refer the patient to the hospital chaplain if the patient wishes to discuss spiritual matters which can also involve the ways their religious faith could have an impact upon their recovery process.

# Conclusion

"Non nobis solum nati sumus."
(*Not for ourselves alone are we born.*)
MARCUS TULLIUS CICERO, DE OFFICIIS BOOK 1:22

GETTING SOMEONE TO SPEAK in the form of presentations for over twelve years to groups of medical students and nursing staff, a person who was largely, practically, non-verbal, this is a testimony to the great compassion and patience of one psychiatric department for a mental patient who thought it might be helpful for others to hear her story. Granted, this was a part of medical school education—a class where I told the story of my mental illness along with the recovery process, a mental illness that devastated a large part of my life. For a listing of these presentations please see: https://hopeforrecovery.com/presentations/[1]

The side effects from being given a major psychiatric diagnosis when I was in my twenties has continued to play a part as stigmatization and mistreatment coming from relatives, social groups, the surrounding community, and major institutions. This has gone on far into the days of my mid-to-late adult years. Prejudice hurts. People give unkind glances; people speak unkind words or use harsh tones of voice. It goes on and on, everywhere, every place, ignorance reigns. Discrimination is based on ignorance and the

1. Murphy, *Presentations*.

kind of worldview that does not respect difference. Neurodiversity, or difference in mental abilities are a new development in diversity studies but far too many people have no interest in the content of this field of study. For a more detailed reflection on the topic of the broad side effects of a diagnosis please see my previous work, *To Loose the Bonds of Injustice: The Plight of the Mentally Ill and What the Church Can Do*.[2]

Even as a neurodivergent (or special needs) individual I felt I had a mission to tell what God said to me in the rain. Since speaking out loud has been a constant struggle, I put my words down on paper. Lots of words and books later, I developed social skills. Only starting in my fifties did I feel confident to engage socially with others in my church and surrounding community. I can now freely communicate. It's about time, because I still have lots to say.

A person with my diagnosis of schizophrenia can still make positive contributions to the world. People with mental illness can significantly improve their quality of life by turning to God and finding meaningful work. I will share a brief summary of what I've done over the course of my life, not to brag, but to describe how turning to God, to worship God, pray, and belong to a church, can significantly improve a person's productivity and quality of life. By turning to God for guidance and infusion of strength, I am able to do things that have value. Here is a short history of my ministry work and mission efforts. May this work point to God and bring glory to God. I could only do this with God's help and provision of strength. *Such confidence we have through Christ before God. Not that we are competent in ourselves to claim anything for ourselves, but our competence comes from God.* (2 Cor 3: 4–5 NIV).

At the age of eleven my best friend lost her dad to suicide. I took a Bible verse and created a home-made sympathy card for her. This friend and I last communicated in our sixties, in social media.

Around the age of sixteen I decided to wear a pair of moccasins that had holes in the bottom, to school one day. It was freezing cold weather with ice and snow, and I said to myself that I wanted to see how the poor felt. Also, a little later, around the age

---

2. Murphy, *Loose the Bonds*, 79.

## CONCLUSION

of seventeen, I wrote a book of poems, essays, and songs. It was a homemade booklet with tiny spirals and folder/pages including colored illustrations I painted in watercolor.

After the cult years, in my late twenties, I attended a mental health center with a clubhouse model for patients to drop-in to socialize and have coffee. I volunteered to be a contributing editor for the clubhouse newsletter. I did some writing on spirituality then in my thirties and purchased a metal filing cabinet for home use for organizing my compositions. I attended some writing classes and enrolled in a course on philosophy at the University of Iowa. About this time, two counselors from the center started the city's free lunch program open to the public. I took part on the first day offering of the free lunch by helping set-up and serve. Many homeless and poor still attend this and over the years the lunch program has developed into a very big operation with many organizations serving.

At one point, I purchased and took new towels to the Iowa City homeless shelter (Shelter House) for the guests to use with bathing. Later, I did volunteer work at the Domestic Violence Shelter for women and children on and off for about four years. It seemed to me that I felt an internalize sense of justice and I wanted to advocate for those suffering from oppression. I was a survivor of domestic violence and wanted to help others in similar situations.

My current ministries are known as programs of Saint Andrew Presbyterian Church in Iowa City, Iowa. Since I am a survivor of mental difficulties I felt that I could advocate for others so afflicted. Maybe I could help one or several people. So the formal beginning for the Mental Health Initiatives (MHI) program was with my first article published in a professional psychiatric journal in 1997. Later on, I founded the Group for the Advancement of Mental Health (GAMH) in March 2024.

At the suggestion of my psychiatrist and at the age of forty-nine, I started my volunteer work at the University of Iowa Hospitals and Clinics (UIHC) in the Patients' Library. There I did ordinary tasks and duties in the library. Later on outside of library work, I did presentations for UIHC psychiatric nursing staff and medical students going through their psychiatry rotation (with

PowerPoint slideshows). The talks were about my experience with mental illness and recovery story. I hoped that by sharing my story that the listeners might gain an appreciation of how spirituality is an important factor in recovery. I also did a presentation for the UI Psychology Department (doctoral students) and at Coe College in Cedar Rapids for psychiatric nursing students. I also spoke at churches of different denominations. I did talks until my physical health disability prevented it after about twelve years.

I created a few videos and other materials for education of psych department in-patient staff at the hospital and provided information for patients in the in-patient units, like how to find the free lunch upon discharge. I wrote a series of very small grants to obtain comfort items for the psych in-patients, once a used player piano for a psych ward; and other things like CD players, headphones, and CDs. I delivered magazines once a week to the psych units and the out-patient clinic waiting room. As I started to communicate with the nurse managers of the psych units to find out the patients' needs, I arranged to do on-going clothing and magazine drives at my church several times a year and I delivered them to the hospital for the psych wards. This developed into a permanent program for providing low-income psych patients' clothing, shoes, and other items like weighted blankets. When they renovated the child psych unit's patio they put up a plaque on the wall with my name on it, saying my volunteer hours at the hospital provided funding for the reconstruction.

In addition to MHI beginning in 2013, I began the AIM program (Access & Inclusion Mission) for the disabled in my church and surrounding community with the long-distance guidance of the Rev. Dr. Timothy H. Little of Sacramento, California. I met him at a conference. He was in his seventies and had been blind most of his life, but he was still able to reach the level of director of chaplains at the Davis Medical Center in California while specializing in psychiatry. He guided me on-line and made two trips to St. Andrew where he preached and spoke at workshops I organized. I wrote about him and the history of his work in AIM ministry in a handbook for the guidance of those who wish to begin a disability

## Conclusion

ministry. This booklet is available for download at my website and is in printed form in my Collected Writings book publication.[3]

With Rev. Dr. Little's guidance, I asked and received permission from the hospital administration to begin a spirituality support group at the hospital for a psych in-patient unit. The hospital required that I have a staff chaplain as my partner on the unit during the support group meetings. We attended the meetings together and took turns guiding the group sessions. Starting around 2014 I worked at the Presbytery level (Presbytery of East Iowa, PEIA, Presbyterian Church USA) and was titled the Moderator for the AIM ministries in the PEIA. I wrote and obtained grant funding on numerous occasions, held workshops, and attended a conference. My local AIM group membership extended beyond my church to a staff/librarian of the UI Disability Library and members of other local churches.

All the while these events and activities went on I progressed to the level of part-time volunteer statistician for the Patients' Library, and continued to write articles. I published my first book in 2010, a memoir: *Voices in the Rain: Meaning in Psychosis*.[4] My church work which is elaborated on at my personal website: https://hopeforrecovery.com/)[5] describes things I've done for over two decades. Explore the links and pages of my website to get a better idea of the extent of my continuous work. My book publications are listed in the Appendix for up to the year 2024.

In some of my books I've described my ministry work with more detail than what I've done here. Here in this book I've touched upon some main points. Since I retired from work in the Patients' Library I've been focusing on other things like writing books, holding ministry events, and creating new initiatives. I hope that the work I have done (and hope to continue) can bring awareness to the world of the importance of faith in recovery from mental illness and bring glory to God. Religious faith (or a relationship with

---

3. Murphy, *Collected Writings*, 94–106.
4. Murphy, *Voices in the Rain*.
5. Murphy, *Hope For Recovery*.

## Concerning the Importance of God for Mental Health

God) is a powerful influence in long-term cognitive, emotional, and behavioral outcomes.

The generosity of the missionaries mentioned in Section Two who gave of their time, who sacrificed comforts, and emotionally took on the suffering of other human beings cannot be overlooked. These missionaries risked their lives to help others in need. Concerning the importance of God for mental health these numerous examples of healthy human beings who did missionary work shows how religious faith (or a relationship with God) is a powerful influence in long-term cognitive, emotional, and behavioral outcomes. Good mental health can be described as loving God and neighbor; and the extent to which this is made evident is the degree of mental health a person embodies. As Clinebell said: *A person is mentally healthy to the degree that he is able to live the two great commandments, to love God and neighbor fully.*[6]

So, good mental health is the goal. How do I strive for good mental health daily? What fortifies me to face the challenges that I come across in the normal course of living? The Bible, as holy scripture is key. My view of the Bible is influenced by one of my former advisors, Phil Cary, theologian, author, and Prof Emeritus of Eastern University. Concerning the topic of translations, he says that he believes in the Holy Spirit, whose work on Pentecost shows that the Gospel can thrive in translation.[7] I enjoy my current Bible that has this long title (I found it used, and ordered online several years ago): The Oxford Annotated Bible, revised standard version (RSV), college edition. For a while I read the NIV, then the ESV. Now I mostly read the RSV.

Every morning with my coffee I enjoy a quiet time and read my Bible. If I had the facilities and staff I would conduct research to show how reading the Bible consistently, on a daily basis, will transform the biochemistry of the brain, so much so, as to build a healthy brain. Brain cells of someone who has a mental illness will be repaired and rebuilt which will influence a strong logical functioning and creativity of the mind. The mind (immaterial) and brain

---

6. Clinebell Jr., "Mental Health Through the Religious Community," 34.

7. Phil Cary, email to author, 1/15/2025

(physical) interact, of course. So, starting my day with this exercise of scripture reading is foundational to peace of mind and productivity.

The reason I believe that the Bible has this miraculous power of healing the brain is because I think the Bible is God's word and supernatural message to us. God's miraculous power is made manifest in the words—so this is God communicating to me every day when I read the scriptures. Among other things, I can learn God's commandments, my failures to comply and need of forgiveness, the need to repent. Much guilt can accumulate in a person's life; and the emotional burden can be great. This is why one aspect of good mental health comes from repentance along with a fresh, new beginning.

I seek direction from God. God speaks to me in scripture about what I should do with my life. The Old Testament (OT) shows me the depth of God's ways with us. I do not ignore the OT. I feel it is essential reading along with the New Testament (NT). Once a pastor said to me: "Just read the NT." Wrong!! I learn a lot by reading the stories and narrative text in the OT and what God is saying there. The Gospel is uplifting in parts but also shows us how God holds us accountable to do his will: Jesus said that we are to deny ourselves and pick up our cross: *And he said to all, "If any man would come after me, let him deny himself and take up his cross daily and follow me.* (Luke 9:23 RSV)

As far as arguing with people about various interpretations: Some verses seem clear. Others, are not. I try not to base my conclusions on personal whims; though, I admit, I do have some pretty strong opinions. I cannot function without reading the Bible daily. I become mentally ill without it. Just like church attendance: I can only be sane by attending church. Saint Augustine said that a person has to go into not just the church building, but into the sanctuary where worship is done. We need to be in the sanctuary. And I find this usually true.

Along with reading scripture I have to pray the Lord's Prayer every morning or I will have an extremely bad day. I need God like the air I breathe. Prayer helps with this. Sometimes, I'm rushed, so that's bad; but usually not. I usually pray, additionally, about other things besides the Lord's Prayer. My prayers can last from a few minutes to much longer and it varies daily.

## Concerning the Importance of God for Mental Health

So, scripture, prayer, church: these three. My mental health depends on these.

I began this book by referring to the current research in major universities where work is being done to find the genetic basis of exceptional outcomes in a person's character or personality, talents and achievements, along with good physical health. I want to caution the reader that this is not new. Hitler and the Nazi scientists also had this in mind when they were striving to create the Master Race. Eugenics is still alive and well in the modern world i.e., get rid of the weak and disabled. Proliferate the strong and healthy. Eugenics has a total and reckless disregard for human dignity of people in all shapes and forms. Eugenics in our modern times is still trying to eliminate those who are different or weak; those who need assistance. But keep in mind that those same scientists and hospital staff who are involved in eugenics research may someday by accidental injuries or old age become disabled themselves. Then who will prevent their elimination, as they have not done for others? Will anyone hear their own cries for mercy?[8]

So I maintain that it is religion, theology, and faith which identifies the moral stance needed to support all kinds of life forms, including those with Down syndrome, quadriplegia, and other such disabling conditions. It is God who calls us by name and says: *I made you and you are good.* We are God's creatures, made in God's image. A eugenics scientist denies God and reduces the human being to a financial figure: what are they worth in monetary terms? How can they contribute monetarily to society?

Basing our lives on money will ultimately become boring and empty. Searching for a spiritual meaning with purpose and value will ultimately satisfy. Instead of how much money can I accumulate; it will be how can I give more to help others in need? The importance of God for mental health cannot be over-stated. Often it is a matter of life and death; not only for the self, but also for others in our communities, country, and world. I pray that you, the reader, will grow in spiritual wisdom and the knowledge of God.

---

8. Murphy, *Collected Writings*, 70–78.

# Appendix

## Further Reading

### Books by Marcia A. Murphy
### Founder, Mental Health Initiatives/Group for the Advancement of Mental Health

Murphy, Marcia A. *Knitting with Barbed Wire: Understanding the Factor of Religion in Mental Illness & Health.* Eugene: Resource Publications, an imprint of Wipf & Stock Publishers, 2024.

    Author's book webpage: Knitting With Barbed Wire: Understanding the Factor of Religion in Mental Illness & Health by Marcia A. Murphy

Murphy, Marcia A. *The Compassionate Psychiatrist: Redefining Mental Healthcare.* Eugene: Resource Publications, an imprint of Wipf & Stock Publishers, 2024.

    Author's book webpage: The Compassionate Psychiatrist by Marcia A. Murphy

## Appendix

Murphy, Marcia A. *Homeless: The Unbefriended Poor.* Eugene: Resource Publications, an imprint of Wipf & Stock Publishers, 2023.

    Author's book webpage: Homeless

Murphy, Marcia A. *Schizophrenia & Suicide: Finding Hope, Meaning, and Direction.* Eugene: Resource Publications, an imprint of Wipf & Stock Publishers, 2023.

    Author's book webpage: Schizophrenia & Suicide: Finding Hope, Meaning, and Direction by Marcia A. Murphy

Murphy, Marcia A. *A Small Handbook of Mental Health: Portal to a New Life.* Eugene: Resource Publications, an imprint of Wipf & Stock Publishers, 2022.

    Author's book webpage: Small Handbook of Mental Health

Murphy, Marcia A. *Reflections on the Meaning of Mental Integrity: Recovery from Serious Mental Illness.* Eugene: Resource Publications, an imprint of Wipf & Stock Publishers, 2021.

    Author's book webpage: https://wipfandstock.com/9781666708899/reflections-on-the-meaning-of-mental-integrity/

Murphy, Marcia A. *The Collected Writings of Marcia A. Murphy: Christus Magnus Medicus Sanat (Christ, the Great Physician, Heals).* Eugene: Resource Publications, an imprint of Wipf & Stock Publishers, 2020.

    Author's book webpage: https://hopeforrecovery.com/collected-writings/

Murphy, Marcia A. *To Loose the Bonds of Injustice: The Plight of the Mentally Ill and What the Church Can Do.* Eugene: Resource Publications, an imprint of Wipf & Stock Publishers, 2018.

    Author's book webpage: https://www.hopeforrecovery.com/to-loose-the-bonds-of-injustice/

FURTHER READING

***Allbooks Review International Editor's Choice Award for 2011 Finalist***
Murphy, Marcia A. *Voices in the Rain: Meaning in Psychosis.* Cedar Rapids, IA: Eagle Book Bindery, 2010. Eugene: Wipf & Stock Publishers, Reprint 2018.

Author's book webpage: https://www.hopeforrecovery.com/voices-rain-meaning-psychosis/

# Bibliography

Cary, Phillip. *The Nicene Creed: An Introduction.* Bellingham, WA: Lexham, 2023.

Clinebell Jr., Howard J. "Mental Health Through Christian Community." *Pastoral Psychology* 20, no. 5 (1969) 34.

Cook, Chris C.H. *Hearing Spiritual Voices: Medieval Mystics, Meaning and Psychiatry.* London: T&T Clark, 2023.

Murphy, Marcia A. *The Collected Writings of Marcia A. Murphy: Christus Magnus Medicus Sanat (Christ, the Great Physician, Heals).* Eugene: Resource, 2020.

———. *The Compassionate Psychiatrist: Redefining Mental Healthcare.* Eugene: Resource, 2023.

———. "Having Tea with Anne Hutchinson: Justice, Four Centuries Later." https://hopeforrecovery.com/having-tea-with-anne-hutchinson-justice-four-centuries-later/

———. *Homeless: The Unbefriended Poor.* Eugene: Resource, 2023.

———. "Hope For Recovery." https://hopeforrecovery.com/

———. *Knitting with Barbed Wire: Understanding the Factor of Religion in Mental Illness & Health.* Eugene: Resource, 2024.

———. "Presentations." https://hopeforrecovery.com/presentations/

———. *Reflections on the Meaning of Mental Integrity: Recovery from Serious Mental Illness.* Eugene: Resource, 2021.

———. *To Loose the Bonds of Injustice: The Plight of the Mentally Ill and What the Church Can Do.* Eugene: Resource, 2018.

———. *Voices in the Rain: Meaning in Psychosis, a Memoir.* Eugene: Resource, 2018 (Reprint), Cedar Rapids, IA: Eagle Book Bindery, 2010.

Norton, Michael. "Coup Attempt Thwarted." *Marysville Appeal-Democrat.* December 18, 2001.

www.ingramcontent.com/pod-product-compliance
Lightning Source LLC
LaVergne TN
LVHW051708080426
835511LV00017B/2801